THE HEYDAY OF THE RT

KEVIN McCORMACK

Ian Allan
60th
ANNIVERSARY

Front cover: The 300 Saunders-bodied RTs were well built, but body panels were non-standard and becoming harder to obtain, hence the decision to dispose of these buses before the Park Royal- or Weymann-bodied examples. In this June 1968 shot, RT1939 is about to enter London Bridge bus station. *John Bishop*

Back cover: This close-up of RT4497 at Dorking in April 1969 illustrates the high standard of upkeep enjoyed by the country fleet, even to the extent of the bonnet being repainted when fading (due to heat) began to occur. *Dave Brown*

Title Page: Red and green RTs mingled regularly in several suburban locations well into the 1970s. In the summer of 1973, RT3964 on route 65 and RT4344 on local service 468 pose, along with the author's wife, at Chessington Zoo. *Author*

Right: Here is a treat for David Thrower, owner of much-travelled RTL1050, which now gives rides at the East Anglia Transport Museum, Carlton Colville. Purchased from LT by Pioneer Coaches of Richmond, Surrey, the vehicle is entering a French campsite in August 1967 *en route* to Juan Les Pins on the Mediterranean. The occasion was a three-week camping holiday organised by the Double Decker Club, and a great time was had by all! *Author*

Far right: Numerically the third-earliest country bus in the class, RT599 approaches Wrotham (pronounced 'Rootam') in June 1969. *Dave Brown*

First published 2002

ISBN 0 7110 2927 X

Published by Ian Allan Publishing
an imprint of Ian Allan Publishing Ltd, Hersham, Surrey
KT12 4RG.

Printed by Ian Allan Printing Ltd, Hersham, Surrey
KT12 4RG.

Code: 0210/B2

Introduction

Here is another book celebrating the famous RT bus and its Leyland variants — a bus frequently reviled by enthusiasts in the 1950s and 1960s when it monopolised the towns and villages within a 30-mile radius of the City of London (and the City itself), yet revered in the 1970s as it soldiered on in declining numbers and careworn condition, maintaining standards of reliability which the new generation of one-person-operated ('OPO') vehicles were unable to match.

This volume is not intended to provide an in-depth analysis of the RT class. Readers requiring more detail are recommended to search out my earlier book, *Glory Days: RT*, published by Ian Allan in 1998 and still available. The definitive work, Ken Blacker's *RT — The Story of a London Bus*, published by Capital Transport, is sadly out of print.

The Heyday of the RT is a pictorial tribute in colour to the various types making up the massive total of 6,956 RT-family buses built for London Transport ('LT') between 1939 and 1954. The scarcity of early colour material and the desire to avoid, with only a couple of exceptions, the use of previously published photographs has limited the start date to 1955. From page 4 onwards, the pictures are displayed in approximate chronological order, ending with the final routes which lasted until 1978/9.

The RT was essentially a London bus. Only two other operators took delivery of new RTs: St Helens Corporation with 40 and Coventry Corporation with one. However, redundant London buses from the RT family found purchasers all over Britain and around the world. A handful of photographs have been included which show these vehicles outside London, but the primary objective has been to record these buses in LT red and Lincoln green — and from 1970 in the livery of London Country Bus Services ('LCBS'), successor to LT's Country Bus & Coach Department. It is true that a few RTs have touched the London area over the years since 1979 with other operators but not on a regular, prolonged basis, and such operations are not sufficiently nostalgic to be included here. London's Transport Museum's operational example (RT4712), which has been operating on routes in London in the summer of 2002 to celebrate HM The Queen's Golden Jubilee, is similarly excluded, although it makes a splendid sight in its gold livery.

As regards the photographs themselves, this title has enabled me to dig out more than just my normal token contribution but still relies heavily on the material of others. I am most grateful for the willingness of the following photographers to lend me their precious transparencies: Michael Furnell, Dave Brown, Bruce Jenkins, the late Mike Harries, John Bishop, Marcus Eavis, James Whiting of Capital Transport, Dave Edwards, Geoff Rixon, John Aldridge, Roy Hobbs, Nick Lera, John May, Vernon Murphy, Trevor Saunders and John Webb.

The RT family represented the pinnacle in terms of standardisation and mass production for a single bus operator. Fortunately, it was an outstanding vehicle in terms of design and performance, gracing the streets of London for 40 years. Although the Routemaster ('RM') has already exceeded the RT's record of longevity in LT service, there is a large body of enthusiasts committed to ensuring that the RT family is not forgotten, and I hope these pages will help to keep alive the memory of this faithful workhorse.

Kevin R. McCormack
Ashtead, Surrey
July 2002

Left: It is April 1955 and, with little over a month to go before withdrawal from passenger service, prewar RT42 from Putney (Chelverton Road) garage shelters from the sunlight in Kensington Church Street. *Bruce Jenkins*

Above: Seven prewar RTs received a public-service life extension of just over two years due to a weak bridge at Broxbourne in Hertfordshire, over which route 327 passed. The RTs replaced postwar STLs which were saleable on the second-hand market. Until it was strengthened in 1957, the bridge was unable to take the heavier postwar RT. The prewar RTs were sometimes used on other routes, as depicted here by RT114 at Sele Farm Estate, Hertford, in October 1956. *Bruce Jenkins*

Above: Prewar RT137 heads for the Gate to the enclosure into which stray cattle were put in olden days. This is Lower Nazeing in Essex, at the junction of Middle Street and Hoe Lane (a short cut to the Gate). Still extant today are the house ('Wheelers', *c*1800), the railings alongside the brook and the bus stop, now crumbling in a hedge. RT137 rejoined its red class-mates on training and staff-bus duties on 1 September 1957. *Author's collection*

Right: One of LT's less inspired decisions was to order 120 RT bodies from the Cravens Railway Carriage & Wagon Co. Apart from the cab and front wings, the bodies were completely non-standard. The order was placed because bus body availability was not keeping pace with chassis production. However, by the time the Cravens RTs had been delivered (some 18 months late), the problem had resolved itself. In June 1955, shortly before withdrawal, RT1498 was photographed at Southfields station, operating the Wimbledon Tennis Championships service. *Bruce Jenkins*

Above: Due to over-ordering (because service reductions had not been anticipated), there were too many RTs. The axe fell on the Cravens-bodied buses, which did not fit into the Aldenham overhaul programme involving the interchange of bodies and chassis. This variant was withdrawn between June 1955 and October 1956, and these comparatively new vehicles were quickly snapped up. RT1418 went to a Scottish operator, Lowland of Shettleston, where it was photographed in July 1956. *Bruce Jenkins*

Right: Illustrating the dark blue blinds associated with limited-stop express services is RT3141, standing alongside TD106 at Kingston station in the summer of 1957. *John Webb*

Above: In order to release into service brand-new RTs and RTLs which were gathering dust in storage, LT decided to sell off some of its earlier standard postwar RTs and RTLs. RTL49 went to Scottish operator A. & C. McLennan, which fitted platform doors. This scene was recorded in Perth in July 1959. *Bruce Jenkins*

Right: Shortly before the addition of trafficator 'ears', RT282, a recipient of a later body following an Aldenham overhaul, stands beside trolleybus No 1567 at Lea Bridge depot in 1959. Route 661 was withdrawn on 18 August 1959. *Marcus Eavis*

Above: Red Rover Omnibus was one of several buyers of redundant RTs which tried to modernise the appearance of the older bodies by removing the roofbox. A typical example is RT423, depicted here at Aylesbury in 1959. *Marcus Eavis*

Right: Photographed alongside TD105 at Edgware station in July 1961 is RT554, with early bodywork. The use of offside route stencil plates ceased in late 1963/early 1964. *John Bishop*

Left: Possibly the closest there was to a single-deck RT was the postwar AEC Regal (T class) with Mann Egerton bodywork. The last of the class to remain in service, T787, stands at Crawley garage alongside RT4171 in May 1962, three months before withdrawal. *John Bishop*

Below: Devoid of its radiator badge, RTL1456 pulls out of Hainault Street into Ilford High Road on 30 June 1962. Route 169A was a new service absorbing routes 663 and 691, upon implementation of Stage 3 of the trolleybus-replacement programme on 19 August 1959. *Trevor Saunders*

Left: This view at Moorgate in June 1962 provides another reminder of the trolleybus-replacement era as early-bodied RT697 arrives at the City terminus of route 21. *Nick Lera*

Below: RTs were capable of many things, but not passing under low bridges (although a few tried!). LT purchased 76 low-height Regents for this purpose. The rather old-fashioned shape of RLH14 contrasts with the sleek lines of RT2010 contemplating a trip to Kew Gardens on route 90. This view is at Staines West station, probably in the summer of 1963. *John May*

Left: RTs were a pleasure to behold even from the rear! RT1817 travels along Petersham Road, Richmond, beneath Star & Garter Hill, in June 1964. *Mike Harries*

Above: Perhaps the finest of all the RTs when they were smartly turned out were the Green Line examples, with their raised bullseye motifs, special fleetnames and absence of posters. RT4496 belongs to a batch of 21 of these vehicles which emerged in 1954 carrying former SRT bodies. *James Whiting*

Above: The extra width (6in) of the RTWs was a bonus in peak periods because it created more gangway space, but drivers disliked the class because of excessive noise and heavy steering. RTW21 is depicted in Greenland Road, Camden, in January 1966, a month before the RTWs were taken off route 31. *James Whiting*

Right: The last of the 500 RTWs ran in public service on 14 May 1966 on route 95. Shortly before the end, RTW494 was photographed outside Brixton garage. *James Whiting*

Left: RT1336 reverses into the popular terminus outside the Royal Forest Hotel, Chingford, in October 1966. The bus has received a recent overhaul and has the new pale grey central relief band, a livery change introduced the previous year. RT2460 is on the right. *Robin Hannay collection*

Above: In this unusual view of an RT parked 'end-on' at a bus station, Hatfield garage's RT3422 stands at Hitchin, one of LT's most northerly outposts, on 25 July 1966. Hitchin used to have a bus garage, which was reconstructed in 1955 to accommodate RTs but nevertheless closed in 1959. *Geoff Rixon collection*

Left: The narrow Leylands (RTLs) outlived their wider contemporaries (the RTWs) by 2½ years in London passenger service. Route 106 lost its RTLs on 7 September 1968. This scene at Clapton depicts RTL1018. *John Bishop*

Above: Bus preservation is not a new phenomenon and began to gain momentum in the mid-1960s. The LT contingent at this school fête near Uxbridge in the summer of 1967 comprises Cravens RT1431, RTL1323 (masquerading as a Green Line RTL) and T792. At this time, LT would not permit any sold vehicles to carry the London Transport fleetname. *Author*

Left: In the days before Victoria station received a covered bus station, RTL1514 (minus its radiator badge) heads a line-up that includes a Strachans-bodied Merlin and an early RM. The date is 23 May 1968. *Bruce Jenkins*

Right: Route 10 also lost its RTLs on 7 September 1968. Two days earlier, RTL506 carefully avoids the photographer somewhere in the City. There were 1,631 RTLs built, but they were less popular with drivers than RTs, and, because of their different mechanical units, it made sense to standardise the remnants of the RT family by retaining the more numerous Park Royal- and Weymann-bodied AECs. LT's RTLs ran for the last time in public service on 29 November 1968. *John Aldridge*

Woodford Bridge
Wanstead Stratford
Aldgate London Bridge
Lambeth Bridge

10

LEYTONSTONE

GONE WITH THE WIND

KXW 289

Above: Next in the firing line after the RTLs were the Saunders-bodied RTs, the last class members with roofboxes. Only one survived in service beyond June 1970 (because it had been fitted with a heater by mistake). In February 1969 RT1061 heads southwards across Waterloo Bridge, regardless of what the destination blind states. *Mike Harries*

Right: For those readers interested in RT roofs, here is a bird's-eye view (from Waterloo Bridge) of RT476. The bus is standing on the Victoria Embankment in February 1969. In the background is Somerset House, designed in the late 1770s as one of the world's first purpose-built office blocks. *Mike Harries*

Above: Red RTs did not come much smarter than RT2986, seen working the under-used 81C service at Heathrow Airport in May 1969. RMs took over this route on 23 August 1969. Any offers for the Austin A35? *Mike Harries*

Right: This fine portrait of Sutton garage's RT2831 was taken alongside Epsom station in the summer of 1969. Note that the offside route stencil holder has been removed and a new panel inserted — treatment which was not applied universally. Route 93 now terminates in Priory Road, Cheam, and the 293 covers the Epsom end. *Roy Hobbs*

Left: In their later days, the Saunders-bodied RTs sometimes acquired rear blinds at the front, thus rendering the roofbox number unnecessary. Demonstrating this feature at Golders Green station in June 1969 is RT2457. *Dave Brown*

Above: Following the arrival of the Routemaster coaches, the Green Line fleet of 85 RTs was whittled down to 23 in 1965 and was finally eliminated in November 1969. In this July 1969 view near Rickmansworth, Green Line RT3647 has been relegated to a bus duty. *Author*

Left: RTs 1380 and 2740 meet at Bromley North. Route 61 was taken over by OPO DMS vehicles on 15 July 1972, but the 146 kept its RTs until 22 April 1978, when conversion to single-deck BLs occurred. *Dave Brown*

Above: 1969 was the final year of LT's country bus and Green Line operations before these were transferred to the newly formed National Bus Company subsidiary, London Country Bus Services. RT964 has left the southeastern suburbs behind as it heads into the Kent countryside in the summer of 1969. *Dave Brown*

Above: Amersham garage's allocation on the long Berkhamstead–Windsor 353 service switched from RTs to OPO Swifts in February 1971, although Windsor still had some scheduled RT workings. While the old order still reigned supreme, RT1076 was photographed leaving Gerrards Cross. *Vernon Murphy*

Right: RT1708 travels along the Strand near Aldwych in June 1970. This is no ordinary RT, however, for it carries the body from RT2776, which toured North America in 1952 giving rides. Extra ventilators were fitted to improve air flow in the hotter states visited. *Bruce Jenkins*

Left: Back to Heathrow again for this June 1969 shot of RT494 entering the Central Terminal Area, and without an aircraft in sight. Route 91 was withdrawn between Hounslow West and the airport on 23 August 1969. *Mike Harries*

Below: When LCBS assumed control of the green fleet on 1 January 1970, nothing much changed for the first few months. RT628 remains much in its LT state in this view at Croydon in June 1970, despite the new fleetname. *Mike Harries*

Left: Most LCBS RTs lost their LT radiator badges immediately in an effort to eradicate the bullseye symbol (yet still visible on the front posters!). LCBS devised its own logo, but this was killed off by the National Bus Company when the latter introduced its corporate image in 1972. Only one RT carried the new logo on its radiator badge — RT1000, seen here at Biggin Hill on 19 September 1970. *Mike Harries*

Right: Now we visit the East End's dockland area for a sight of the Wanstead–North Woolwich 101 service. Pictured on 13 August 1971 near Royal Albert Dock is Upton Park garage's RT2725. The bus is actually passing the Port of London Authority's former Manor Way station, which was closed on 8 September 1940. Beckton gasworks can be seen in the background. *Marcus Eavis*

Left: RTs 3635 and 3665 may look alike, even down to the faded paintwork on the bonnets, but the one on the left has a pale green waistband, identifying it as a former Green Line vehicle. This pair were photographed at Biggin Hill on 18 September 1971. *Mike Harries*

Above: RT688 passes Somerset House on the Victoria Embankment in March 1972 while working a 'short' to visit the Greater London Council bosses. Route 172 was converted to DM operation on 3 August 1975. Until the 1860s, when the Embankment was built, the River Thames lapped against the arches on the left. *Dave Brown*

Left: Struggling up Anerley Hill, near Crystal Palace, in this shot dating from July 1972 is RT3268. Route 157 lost its RTs in favour of DMS Fleetlines on 12 May 1973. *Dave Edwards*

Right: RTs 2128 and 3180 wait at the Woolwich terminus of route 75 in July 1973. This service was converted to DMS operation on 26 February 1977. *Dave Edwards*

Above: In the summer of 1973, RT4117 hurries along Kingston Road, just south of Tolworth, looking very much like an LT vehicle, even down to having a Central Area radiator badge. *Author*

Right: LT's plans to withdraw the RT fleet by 1975 were thwarted by the unreliability of newer buses and, in 1974, a limited recertification and repaint programme began. RT3470 was dealt with at Stonebridge Park garage and is seen on a test run, carrying trade plates. The bus is turning into Harlesden Road, Willesden. *Author*

Left: RT2175 mixes with the shoppers in High Street, Bromley, in June 1974. Route 94 was the third-last regular RT service, albeit with some RM assistance, lasting until 26 August 1978. It was the longest continuously worked RT route, spanning 30 years from 1948 to 1978. *John Bishop*

Above: Two more RT services seen frequenting Bromley in June 1974 were routes 119A and 146. The former served South London urban areas while, in contrast, the latter was mainly a rural route. RT3393 waits as an elderly passenger alights. *John Bishop*

Above: With its destination blind already reset, albeit for a short journey, RT2406 passes Holy Trinity Church, Bromley Common, on 6 November 1974, heading for nearby Bromley garage. Normally travelling through Oxford Street to reach Marylebone, the 1 was one of the last regular RT routes to pass through the West End. RMs took over in early 1975. *Michael Furnell*

Right: Loughton garage, where this view of RTs 652 and 2432 was taken in August 1975, lost its RT allocation on 20 August 1977, when route 217A was withdrawn. Route 20A succumbed to DMS operation on 9 October 1976. *Dave Brown*

Above: The date is 6 April 1975 and RT196 looks remarkably smart for a 1947-built vehicle, although it carries a later body. Route 180A was normally RM-operated when this view was taken at Abbey Wood station. The level crossing was closed on 11 July 1975, when a bypass overbridge was opened. *Michael Furnell*

Right: September 1975 in Charing Cross Road sees RT2839 on a short working of route 176. Walworth and Willesden garages shared this service, which was another of the last central London RT routes, RMs taking over in March 1976. *Dave Brown*

Left: Palmers Green garage continued to field RTs for route 102 through to 4 March 1978, when full conversion to RM operation took place. Here is RT3467 in June 1975 in Albert Road, Muswell Hill. *Dave Brown*

Above: Palmers Green and Walthamstow garages shared RT workings on route 34 until these ceased on 10 September 1977. This view at Arnos Grove dates from June 1975 and depicts RT2061. *Dave Brown*

Left: 1975 was a good year for smart RTs. An example is RT2278, photographed on 23 October 1975 passing a line of condemned houses in Abbey Road. The bus is close to Abbey Wood garage, where this short working will terminate. *Michael Furnell*

Above: LCBS had similar difficulties to LT's in terms of trying to eliminate its RT fleet — a situation made more urgent because of the company's objective of achieving 100% OPO as quickly as possible. RT994 passes through Ongar on 24 March 1976 during the last week of RT operation on route 339. *Michael Furnell*

Left: Signs of desperation on the part of LCBS are evident in this shot of RT3520 with strange blind display at Stevenage on 29 April 1976. Crew-worked RP coaches took over the 303C route on 15 May 1976. *Michael Furnell*

Above: RMs took over operation of Sutton garage's route 164 on 16 January 1977. RT2875 has just crossed the A217 and is proceeding along Fir Tree Road, Banstead, in this view taken on 13 May 1976. *Michael Furnell*

Above: Plumstead garage clung on to its RTs until 22 April 1978, when conversion of route 122 to RM operation took place. On 29 May 1976 RT4422 proceeds along Pickford Lane, Bexleyheath, on a Saturday extension to Slade Green station.
Michael Furnell

Right: RT1566 catches the evening sun in The Oval, Blackfen, on a short working to Sidcup garage on 8 June 1976. Route 51A was withdrawn a year later.
Michael Furnell

Above: Despite LCBS's hiring buses from other operators, its difficulties in finding serviceable vehicles in the mid-1970s continued — a situation exacerbated by a shortage of RM spares. A decreasing number of licensed RTs continued to play their part, as evidenced in this scene at St Albans on 5 August 1976, depicting RT603 passing a stationary Merlin. *Michael Furnell*

Right: Most LCBS RTs received yellow waistbands and lettering to brighten up their appearance. Here is an example, RT4742, receiving a top-up at Godstone garage on 12 August 1976. *Michael Furnell*

Above: Dartford garage found itself short of vehicles in the summer of 1976 and borrowed RT604 from Chelsham. Despite a dented front dome, the bus looks quite presentable as it stands at Joyce Green Hospital, Dartford, on 18 August 1976. *Michael Furnell*

Right: During the twilight years from 1976 to 1979, there were still some RT surprises to come. The first, arising from a temporary surplus of recertified RTs, was their unexpected use on routes which had not seen the class for years or — as in the case of Leyton garage's route 230 — ever. RT531 stands in the old Stratford bus station in March 1977. *Bruce Jenkins*

Above: What better to lead the parade of silver buses painted to celebrate HM The Queen's Silver Jubilee than a newly overhauled RT? The last repainted RT to enter LT service, RT1599 sets off from Hyde Park on Easter Sunday, 10 April 1977. RT4712 would perform a similar role for Her Majesty's Golden Jubilee in 2002. *Michael Furnell*

Right: A few days before Sidcup garage's route 228 was converted to RM operation on 21 May 1977, RT2944 was photographed at Chiselhurst Common, heading for the now defunct Well Hall station. *Michael Furnell*

Left: Short-lived joy came to bus enthusiasts in the spring of 1977 when LCBS unexpectedly recertified four RTs to cover vehicle shortages, repainting three of them in NBC leaf green. RT3461 re-entered service in May 1977 at Chelsham garage and was photographed the following month at West Croydon bus station. Sadly it became a trainer in September 1977 and only one of the quartet (RT604) survived in public service for more than a year (until September 1978). *Author*

Above: The last RT routes were well spread out. School children throng the pavement in this early-morning shot in Western Road, Southall, in March 1978 which features a numerically early specimen, RT206, with another RT in pursuit. Shepherds Bush and Southall garages lost their RT allocations when route 105 was converted to RM operation on 30 April 1978. *Author*

Left: It's lighting-up time at Beaconsfield — at least in the cab of the RT! With the last Aldenham overhauls having occurred (and five-year Certificates of Fitness issued) in 1972, all the remaining LCBS RTs (19 at the end of 1976) were due to come off the road by April 1977. One such vehicle was RT1009, still active here on 14 February 1977. *Michael Furnell*

Right: Here is a shot of Enfield garage's route 135 — a late conversion to RM operation, on 16 January 1978. Thirteen days earlier, RT4627 stands outside Brimsdown station. *Michael Furnell*

Above: Considering this photograph was taken as late as February 1978, Kingston garage deserves praise for the smart appearance of RT2816. The bus is leaving Surbiton on its way to the terminus at LCBS's Leatherhead garage. RMs took over the following month. *Geoff Rixon*

Right: The glut of operational RTs in 1975/6 became a famine in 1978, and LT was forced to extract RTs from the training fleet to put back into passenger service. There was great excitement when an assortment of privately owned RTs and RTLs were hired as replacement trainers. RT2553, photographed entering Chiswick Works in late April 1978, was one of several early roofbox models welcomed by LT. *Author*

Left: Undertaking the Sunday-afternoon 'graveyard slot' in June 1978 is Harrow Weald garage's RT3220, passing Cherry Lane cemetery in Shepiston Lane, Hayes, on its way to picking up the M4 spur to Heathrow. RMs took over from RTs, virtually unannounced, on 15 July 1978. *Author*

Above: Problems with a narrow bridge at Chadwell Heath station on route 62 delayed withdrawal of the last RTs until 1979, by which time only a few survivors had current Certificates of Fitness. RT379 presents a rather forlorn sight as it travels along Whalebone Lane North, between Hainault and Chadwell Heath, in the summer of 1978. *Author*

Left: Barking garage had the honour of operating LT's last RTs in passenger service. RT3911 passes through Barking on 24 September 1978. The 87 was the penultimate RT route and was converted to RM operation (apart from one Saturday RT allocation) on 28 October 1978. *Geoff Rixon*

Above: Doomsday arrives at 1.45pm on Saturday 7 April 1979 at Barking garage as RT624 completes the final service journey of a London Transport RT. Can you spot yourself among the crowd witnessing the end of an era? *Bruce Jenkins*